THE POLITICAL ECONOMY OF MIGRANT LABOUR

Shankar Gopalakrishnan
and
Priya Sreenivasa

In Association with

ŚRUTI

Society for Rural Urban & Tribal Initiative

The Political Economy of Migrant Labour
by Shankar Gopalakrishnan and Priya Sreenivasa

First Published, 2009

ISBN 978-93-5002-011-1

Published by
AAKAR BOOKS
28 E Pocket IV, Mayur Vihar Phase I, Delhi-110 091
Phone : 011-2279 5505 Telefax : 011-2279 5641
aakarbooks@gmail.com; www.aakarbooks.com

In association with
SRUTI
Q-1, Hauz Khas Enclave, New Delhi-110 016
Web : www.sruti.org.in
E-mail : sruti@vsnl.com

Printed at
Sapra Brothers, Noida

Contents

Introduction **5**
Structure of This Booklet 6
Chapter I : The Site of Origin **9**
The Agrarian Situation 10
Peasants as Workers: The "Employment" Problem 11
Debt 15
Caste Relations 16
Gender: Relations Between Women, Men and Migration 18
Migration and Socioeconomic Impacts at the Site of Origin 21
References 24
Chapter II : The Site of Destination **26**
Some Types of Worksites 26
Characteristics of the Worksites 28
Structures of Exploitation of Migrant Workers 30
Labour Relations at the Worksites 34
References 35
Chapter III : The Process of Migration **36**
Recruitment of Migrant Workers 36
The Impact of the Migration Process on Collective Action 39
References 41
Chapter IV : The Larger Social Formation **42**
Creating a Reserve Army of Labour: Transitions in Agriculture 42

Finding Work in a Distorted Economy 47
Migration As A Force for *"Disorganising"* Labour 49
References 51
Conclusion **52**
Bibliography **55**

Introduction

Throughout large parts of rural India, among a large part of our adult population, employment and work means leaving their homes: forever, for years, or seasonally every year. For many adivasis and Dalits in particular, migration has long been a central livelihood strategy. While no one, including the government, has any figures for overall migration, estimates say that around one to three crore people engage in seasonal migration alone every year.

Yet, despite such a central place for migration in people's livelihoods and in the economy of the country, there is a surprising lack of information, policies and political focus on the issue. Across India's political spectrum, most forces share the assumption that migration is an "aberration", a problem created by a lack of livelihoods in rural areas. In this view, migration is something to be stopped, a social "evil" that can be eradicated if only sufficient steps are taken to improve the situation in agriculture.

The result is that few in India have engaged with migration as a political phenomenon. Mass movements tend to ignore it in their politics and demands; the state identifies it as a problem, like bonded labour, that is expected to "go away" if all policies are properly implemented; political parties also maintain their silence on the issue, with migration becoming a political battleground only for those who attack migrants from the right wing (such as the Shiv Sena in

Maharashtra and the BJP's campaign against "Bangladeshi" migrants).

But migration in fact plays a central role in India's society and economy, a role that is increasing. Directly or indirectly, many economic activities depend on migrant labour, and in turn its importance as an income source is only rising. This booklet attempts to look at this phenomenon and to understand migrant labour as a part of India's economy. We argue that migration is no aberration, but the result of changes that have transformed large parts of rural India.

Structure of This Booklet

There are many types of migration, driven by different processes and reasons. This booklet focuses on one type of migration in particular, the one most familiar from Dalit and adivasi areas: seasonal migration for work, usually undertaken in the non-agricultural season. Official data on the number of people who undertake such migration does not exist. Census and other surveys are only able to produce reliable figures for longer-term migration, namely those who shift their place of residence entirely. However, as said earlier, estimates place the number of seasonal migrants at between one to three crore adults every year. It is also generally accepted that the number of people involved in seasonal migration is rising[1], in particular over the past two decades. Data from Bihar shows that the proportion of migrant workers increased from 10% of the adult population in 1981-1982 to 19% in 1999-2000[2].

Like any kind of labour, seasonal migration is a process that is produced by, and in turn produces, the social relations of production. There are different levels at which we can examine these relations of production. As a form of mobile labour, though, there are four levels that are particularly relevant for examining seasonal migration. These are as follows:

Site of origin: Many analyses of migration focus on one such level: the site of origin, or the place from which people migrate. The social formation in this area is what produces the immediate need for people to migrate for work, and most struggles against exploitation of migrant labour focus on changing relations in this sphere in order to reduce this perceived need.

Site of destination: Also important, though, is the social formation of the area that people migrate to. Social relations in the site of destination determine who is employed and how, drawing people into the migrant labour cycle and in turn determining the kind of production that their labour contributes to.

Migration process: A third element, though it is not a social formation, it is the process by which migrant labour is recruited. Migration is a highly organised system, involving different actors who together cooperate to make seasonal migration possible. This process also contributes to shaping social relations both at the site of origin and at the site of destination.

The national / regional formation: Finally, all three of these processes are not independent of each other – they are different facets of the larger national and/or regional social formation that creates and defines them. Seasonal migrant labour, we will argue, is not defined purely by local circumstances but is an integral part of much larger national and regional processes in India's society and polity.

Of course, to fully explore each of these areas would require a book in itself. This booklet aims rather at being a very brief sketch, an outline of major areas that are each worthy of more exploration in themselves. At the end, we argue that migration has to be understood as a way of disorganising and disuniting the working class, and hence the exploitation of migrant workers requires us to design strategies aimed at countering this "disorganising" tendency. This booklet does not itself suggest how that can be done;

that will be the subject of a follow on manual on the various policy and legal tools that can be used in this struggle.

This booklet draws on the experience of one of the authors – Priya Sreenivasa - when working in Thane District of Maharashtra with the Kashtakari Sanghatna, as well as on published academic research articles and references. Wherever points or examples are made that are also contained in published research, the concerned article is cited, so as to allow readers to also read further on the issues.

References

1. Deshingkar and Start 2003?, Rogaly 2008.
2. Sharma 2005.

Chapter I

The Site of Origin

Unlike sites of destination, the places from which people migrate in India share one characteristic: they are mostly rural agricultural areas[1]. But, contrary to the general understanding, people do not only migrate from "backward" or marginalised areas. In addition to personal and anecdotal evidence of migration from such areas, case studies by researchers also demonstrate this fact. One study found that at least one member in 15% and 10% of households in two villages in a wealthy region of Andhra Pradesh undertook migration during the year. In Madhya Pradesh, the figures for similarly wealthy villages were much higher – 21% and 43%[2].

Throughout rural India, in other words, people choose to migrate for work, even if they may choose to migrate for shorter periods or for less difficult work in more wealthy areas. The next question is therefore the standard one: why do people migrate? What is it that makes it difficult to secure employment locally? What "pushes" people out of their home areas for work?

These are the basic questions that have dominated most of our discussions on migration, be they in policy documents or in political struggles. This chapter briefly outlines these areas, many of which will be very familiar to those who know the ground reality. In the next three chapters, we will enter into discussions both on the origins of this situation, and on the other, less discussed sociopolitical aspects of migration.

The Agrarian Situation

When talking about migration, we usually begin with the state of agriculture in the area. People migrate, it is argued, because of the failure of their agricultural activities to provide an adequate livelihood. In particular, the lack of land is often pointed out as a major factor in "driving" migration. Most cultivators in India lack sufficient land to survive, while an increasing number have no land at all and have been proletarianised. Inequality in land ownership is rising.

Hence it is not surprising to find that the majority of those who migrate fall within the categories of landless workers and sub-marginal peasants, i.e. those holding very small plots of land. Indeed, one statistical study found that sub-marginal peasants are slightly more likely to migrate on a seasonal basis than landless workers, since they have the initial small savings required to finance migration[3].

The link between migration and landlessness is as true in wealthy areas as in poor ones. Indeed, superficially "prosperous" areas generally mask an acceleration in land loss among poorer peasants, as the penetration of capitalist agriculture leads to more land being concentrated in a few hands. Thus, for instance, in Murshidabad District in Bengal, the creation of irrigation infrastructure and cash crop agriculture – combined with ecological factors such as the shifting of the Padma river, which deprived many of their lands – actually was accompanied by more and more migration as people lost their lands to moneylenders or were cheated out of land by more powerful communities[4].

Similarly, lack of access to irrigation and to finance for agricultural inputs are also among the reasons that people turn to migration. The ability to produce only one crop in a year is insufficient to survive, hence pushing people into migration during the non-agricultural season. Even in areas with generally well developed infrastructure, such irrigation and inputs are usually restricted to the larger farmers.

These conclusions can hardly be disputed, and are

obvious both from the ground reality and from available data. Yet these seemingly simple facts mask a deeper process at work. When one states that agriculture is no longer productive enough to ensure a livelihood, we have to ask what kind of livelihood is required. For this too has changed as much as land inequality has risen.

The most immediate change that one can observe – particularly in adivasi areas – is a steadily rising need for a cash income. The reason why is rooted in larger national processes to which we will return in chapter 4, but it is clear that the earlier systems of resource use and support, which did not require access to money or the market, do not work any longer. Instead, there is a growing dependence on the market for even basic necessities of survival, like clothing, certain food items (e.g. vegetables) etc. This is of course nothing new in itself. This integration with the market has gradually taken place over the last century among all of India's rural population, starting with the nineteenth century and accelerating in the decades after independence[5].

What this means, however, is that the definition of "productive" agriculture has also changed. Agriculture no longer needs to only be productive enough to supply food for the entirety of the year. It now has to produce a *surplus* over and above the food requirements of the family in order to earn sufficient cash to pay for the other requirements of subsistence. But this is a very different requirement, and entails an integration with the market and a productive capacity that automatically excludes most smaller holdings. It is hence not surprising that a survey in the 1980's found that only about 12% of Bhil adivasis in southern Gujarat could sustain themselves on agriculture alone[6].

Peasants as Workers: The "Employment" Problem

In itself this is obvious: the majority of the rural population clearly hires itself out for work at least part of the year. However, if this is the case, then we must look at people as *workers* in addition to, or instead of, only being *peasants*. If this is the case, then the question of employment becomes as critical as access to land and infrastructure.

But employment in rural areas is an equally well known problem. Remunerative employment in rural areas is difficult to come by, especially in marginal areas. As will be argued, this lack of employment is no accident, but is a fundamental feature of the capitalist economy. People are pushed on to the labour market by the dynamics that make it impossible or undesirable for them to survive from agriculture, but there is never sufficient employment to guarantee them survival. The methods by which this happens in rural India include the following:

- The seasonal nature of agricultural employment.
- A lack of capital investment by private capital, for the following among other reasons:
  - ❒ A lack of purchasing capacity among the rural poor; hence private capitalists seeking profits produce for urban elites rather than supplying rural areas.
  - ❒ The lack of infrastructure like roads, transport systems, etc. in many rural areas, which makes production costs in most rural areas higher and leads to concentration of industrial production in areas with such infrastructure (like those close to cities).
  - ❒ A lack of interest on the part of capital in investing in agriculture, meaning that those in possession of sufficient capital (such as landlords etc.) prefer to invest it elsewhere. This has become particularly the case after liberalisation in 1991, when increasing imports and integration with the world market meant that cash crop agriculture is increasingly unprofitable. In other areas, the lack of implementation of land reform laws means that absentee landlords continue to operate, extracting surplus through rents from tenants rather than investing in agriculture itself.

- Declining public investment by the government in rural areas. Given the lack of interest by private capital in rural areas, in India government spending plays a key role. The government hires workers directly for public works. Moreover, higher spending by the government puts more money into the rural economy, builds infrastructure and makes cash crop agriculture more viable, all of which together mean that private capitalists are more interested in investing and hiring workers. But, since liberalisation in 1991, government spending in rural areas has been declining. The result has been an even greater collapse in rural employment. The National Rural Employment Guarantee Scheme is the first change in this tendency.
- A preference by employers for outside migrant labour. In many areas and for many types of work, employers prefer to hire people from outside the local area, as will be explored in the next chapter. Jan Breman (2008) for instance outlines how Gujarati sugar cooperatives preferred to hire employees from Maharashtra rather than the local landless Halpati labourers.

Moreover, in addition to the general lack of employment, there has also been a very visible change in the kind of relations that people have with employers. This shift has happened gradually in most areas between the late 1960's and the present day, corresponding to the penetration of capitalist relations of production deeper and deeper into rural areas and agriculture (see chapter 4). Some of the changes that have taken place in the nature of employment include[7]:

- *A shift from caste-based, personal labour relations to long term contracts:* Workers in rural areas, both in agriculture and outside, were previously hired on the basis of caste and personal connections – often without explicit wages, instead being provided payments in kind and assistance with some services.
- *A shift from open ended, permanent personal relations with one employer to defined contractual obligations:* Earlier

relationships tended to be open ended, without any clear definition of what work was required, in exchange for which the dominant caste member or employer would provide some protection and assistance. For instance, some communities would often specialise in being domestic workers and farm hands for zamindars and landlords, living on the employer's land and dependent on the employer for shelter, assistance and survival; in exchange for which they performed all tasks that were required. Now, workers tend to be hired for one or the other task and paid in cash, with the employer undertaking no obligations beyond paying wages.

- *A shift from using coercion and force to "voluntary" agreements between workers and employers:* Whereas earlier, force was often applied to compel workers to provide their services or to punish those who attempted to escape from employers, current labour relations tend to be more open, subject to negotiation and based – superficially – on the choice of both worker and employer. Employers hold workers to them using money-based mechanisms, such as advances and debt, rather than physical coercion alone.
- *A shift from hiring from within the village to a mix of outside and local labour:* The combination of increased availability of migrant workers together with the preference of employers for migrant workers now means that workers often are hired both from outside and within the village, instead of depending on local labour alone.

All of these changes can be summed up in a single transition – the change from what sociologists describe as "patron-client relations" to formal wage labour relations. In the earlier "feudal" system, the relationship was one of mutual social obligation – landless workers and marginal peasants had to provide their labour and services, in exchange for patronage and support, generally by the zamindar or landlord. In the new relations, as in all such transitions to capitalist relations, there is less coercion but also less security, driving people to migrate in search of wages for survival.

Where it does exist, local employment tends to be seasonal in nature and mostly in the agricultural sector. Here, there is a significant difference depending on the local social structure. Employment is clearly higher in areas which are better "developed", meaning in practice areas where private capital or capitalist farmers have invested in cash crop farming. The survey in Andhra Pradesh quoted earlier found that, on average, households in the two wealthy villages earned Rs. 8672 and Rs. 6692 from employment within the village, of which around 90% was earned from agricultural work. In the same villages families earned only Rs. 224 and Rs. 525 from migrant labour during the year.

Debt

The combination of the need for a cash income with the lack of employment opportunities translates into indebtedness. Loans in this context, however, have multiple implications. Loans from local moneylenders or contractors are tied to other economic activities. For those in a position to produce for sale, loans are often taken from traders or from landlords in exchange for selling them the crop at a reduced rate. For those who work, whether they migrate or not, loans are usually taken as an advance on wages. The latter results in the worker being "tied" to the creditor.

The result of such linkages is the familiar reality of loans becoming a method of extracting an ever-increasing surplus from workers and peasants. The producer is locked into a bond with their moneylender, which may not take the form of actual bonded labour, but means that their freedom to get higher wages and/or higher prices is lost. Lower prices and lower wages result in an inability to repay the loans, or in the need for more loans, in some cases finally ending in actual bondage. Debt therefore becomes a key reason to look for earnings outside – either as a result of generally needing money, or because the loan itself is an advance on wages to be earned during migration.

Caste Relations

In sum, from the above, it is clear that, despite their own variations and the broad variety of areas from which people choose to migrate, there are common features about the social relations that generate the desire or the need to migrate. Those common features extend beyond the realm of strict class relations as well. Two other factors also determine who migrates and how: caste and gender. Both these structures operate across sites of origin and sites of destination, and we will return to them in the following chapters. Here the discussion is limited to their implications for the site of origin and the question of who migrates.

For Dalits and adivasis, lack of access to the means of production – most of these castes are landless workers or marginal producers – is combined with a lack of access to finance and employment. In some areas, these communities are denied certain kinds of work due to straightforward caste discrimination. In others, they are excluded from the work because the work has been "captured" by another community through connections with the employers, which are less likely to exist for these communities[8]. Finally, escaping oppressive caste relations, abuse and violence is one major reason for migration among these communities, though in these cases migration tends to be long term rather than seasonal.

Indeed, Dalits and adivasis form the majority of migrants; a survey among Bhil adivasis in southern Gujarat, for instance, found that over 85% of households depended on migration to survive[9]. In most adivasi areas, it is a familiar sight to find houses and entire villages largely empty during the migration season.

But migration is not limited to Dalits and adivasis, and caste plays a more complex role than only as a "push" factor for oppressed communities. Class dynamics that push people into landlessness and marginalisation may drive other communities to migrate too: in Madhya Pradesh, for instance, one survey in some villages found that 24% of Brahmin households also migrated for work seasonally[10]. But even where people may be compelled to work, how they work and the kind of work they choose is often closely linked to their caste status. Across most upper and middle caste communities in India, as well as those communities who are aspiring to higher caste status, manual work and hiring out of wage labour is considered demeaning.

This has complex implications for migration. Thus, in Bihar, upper castes have been increasingly marginalised by the rise of middle castes such as the Yadavs and Kurmis to greater social power as a result of land reforms and tenancy legislations (see chapter 4); but rather than work locally and diminish their status, these communities often migrate and work elsewhere[11]. In Bengal, where caste relations are less rigid, different communities compete to get a reputation as better "workers", while at the work site the migrant workers tend to feel a common identity across castes[12]. Moreover, caste plays a key role as a network by which people find employment, with employers, contractors, *thekedars* and other workers likely to encourage hiring from within their own community. We will return to this point in the discussion of how migration is organised in chapter 3.

Meanwhile, caste relations themselves are affected by the impact of migration. In the previous section, we noted that the manner in which people relate to their employers is changing. While this in itself is a reason for people to migrate, migration in turn is driving these changes even further. The ability of dominant castes to force work from people, and to practice extreme forms of opppression, is less in areas where migrant labour is a possibility. In Bengal, for instance, the ability of *rajas* – upper caste former zamindars – in parts of Purulia district to hold members of the Bauri community as long term domestic servants (among the women) and farm hands (among the men) has greatly diminished due to migration by these communities to Barddhaman district for work in rice cultivation areas[13]. Similarly, in Bihar, the combination of large scale migration with the Naxalite movement has led to a tightening of the labour market and rising wages for workers, driving upper castes to shift to cultivating their own fields and using family labour[14].

Gender: Relations Between Women, Men and Migration

Migration is also crucially affected by, and in turn affects, the relations between men and women. While the degree to which women migrate varies, there is little doubt that women now form a large section of the agricultural workforce, and indeed are the majority of the rural workforce in the southern States[15]. On the one hand, it is often argued, and to some extent true, that such participation in the workforce has enhanced women's ability to have an independent cash income and hence to resist patriarchal oppression within the household and outside. In reality however the situation is more complex. Oppression of women in this context operates at multiple levels, some of which are briefly outlined here.

Women as the Bearers of "Community Status"

One standard feature of patriarchal systems is the equation of women's conditions with the community's "honour." In many regions, middle castes and Dalits aspiring to higher caste status regard women working or migrating as evidence of lower status for their community as a whole[16]. This tends to discourage both migration and wage labour, and has multiple consequences. In some areas – as for instance is the case in Murshidabad in Bengal – the reluctance to allow women to work resulted in more intense pressure on men to find wage work, leading to more desperation and hence greater insecurity[17]. In others, it leads to women being restricted to lower paid local work, and to restrictions on who they can migrate with, in turn depressing wages and their ability to fight for better working conditions[18].

The Choice to Migrate

Women do however migrate in large numbers. Among adivasi communities, social restrictions on women participating in the workforce are much less. Among other communities, women of poorer households are often compelled to migrate regardless of considerations of status. When such migration does take place, women generally travel along with their husbands, and in most such cases children are also taken along – the family migrates as a unit. Such migration is common for instance in the sugarcane fields of south Gujarat[19], among adivasis in Thane District in Maharashtra and from the Bhil communities of the same area. Such migration tends to be most common among landless households and those without any food or income security during the non-agricultural season, and for whom therefore it would be impossible to leave family members behind. When such migration does take place, as workers the women are frequently at a severe disadvantage. They are always paid less, and in some cases not at all, with the assumption being that the male worker alone is to be paid[20]. Sexual exploitation is extremely common. The next chapter will return to these issues.

In a minority of cases, however, women may migrate alone or in groups. In some cases this is because the work is socially restricted to women: the most obvious example is migration to perform domestic work in others' households, though this is not as such seasonal migration. In other cases, women migrate along established tracks which are known to be "safe" or which are otherwise not 'convenient' for men to migrate on[21] (see below). In some cases, such as cottonseed production in Andhra Pradesh, Gujarat and Karnataka, only children migrated[22].

Connection to Household Work and Responsibility

Whether they participate in migration and work or not, women are generally required to hold sole responsibility for the maintenance of the household and for care of the children. Where women do not migrate, as for instance where the family has sufficient resources to survive without migrating as a unit, or where social restrictions block women's migration, women are then required to maintain the household during the absence of male migrants. The result is a severe strain on women's resources and work. This forces them to take loans from relatives or moneylenders, involving various costs. These costs include committing to low wage "tied" labour[23] or more broadly living up to social and behavioural expectations from family and local powerful communities[24]. Women typically also reduce the amount of food they and the children consume[25]. Where women are unable to obtain local work, their dependence on their husbands increases for cash incomes, reducing their freedom of action within the household and intensifying oppression within the domestic situation.

Greater Difficulties in Organising and in Resistance

All these factors decrease the ability of women to resist exploitation when they do seek work, or when they migrate. Since men enjoy greater freedom of action, the consequences of intensified resistance and organising by men is often not an end to forms of exploitation, but the transfer of those forms of exploitation on to women. Thus, as men resist being "tied" by loans to work for lower wages for certain employers, women have instead been pressurised into taking on such forms of work. This has occurred on a large scale in Andhra Pradesh, where one survey found that women in many cases have been taking on loans independently because of the need to maintain household consumption – and the greater willingness of employers to lend directly to women, in order to secure low wage workers[26]. The survey found that 76% of local women workers participated in such "tied" work relations, as compared to only 56% of men. Such "tying" also includes requirements to perform unpaid work such as cleaning and domestic work, obligations that even men in similar work relationships were not required to undertake.

More generally, as men refuse lower paid wage work and increasingly spend higher disposable income on personal expenses (such as alcohol), the responsibility for household maintenance that women bear often requires them to accept low wage work in order to maintain the household. This is the case in Purulia in Bengal, where low wage local agricultural work is performed by women and adolescents while men await higher wages during migration[27]; and similar situations prevail in Andhra Pradesh[28].

The common pattern is that, like migration itself (as argued in the following chapters), women's labour in conjunction with migration (whether women migrate or not) serves as a means of subsidising others: local capital, capital at the site of destination, contractors, and men in general. This does not mean that migration has no impact on relationships between men and women, and that it cannot at times have a liberating effect. But the overall impact is one of an intensified extraction of surplus from women, with the benefits distributed to different social actors.

Migration and Socioeconomic Impacts at the Site of Origin

In the above two sections we noted some impacts that migration has on caste and gender structures at the site of origin. We have also seen, in brief, how class dynamics can drive people to migrate. This leaves a final question: how does migration in turn impact the overall socioeconomic structure at the site of origin?

There are multiple competing tendencies in this process. On the one hand, in most cases migration does not produce any change in either the class position or the standard of living of migrant workers. Migration is resorted to in the attempt to survive, but the intensity of exploitation in migration is so high that it frequently does no more than allow people to remain alive (and, given its impact on health, often accelerates their death in the long term). Moreover, the close link between migration and indebtedness means that in most cases whatever surplus is earned is extracted by contractors, employers or moneylenders. Migration in such cases is a strategy resorted to because there are literally no options left.

But, on the other hand, this does not mean that migration as such has no impact on the overall social structure. The lack of improvement in the lives of migrant workers should not prevent us from noting the significant changes that take place.

First, as we saw in the discussion on employment, migration is driven in part by changes in the nature of labour relations in rural India. But migration itself also drives such changes. The breakdown of traditional labour relations is accelerated by the ability of both workers and employers to rely on migration as a form of work – for workers because of the increased 'freedom' to enter into wage relationships, and for employers because of the lower costs and easier control over migrant workers[29]. The need for cash may trigger migration in the first place, but over time migration also increases the importance of monetary payments and contractual relationships. Even forms of "unfreedom" that exist in these relationships, such as tying a worker to their contractor through loans, increasingly take on a monetary form.

Alongside such changes, migration also has an "individualising" effect, in a sense more so than other forms of wage labour. The prolonged absence of seasonal migrants from their households and communities reduces the ability to engage in collective decision making at these levels, and instead promotes other senses of identity and solidarity. We noted above the impact that migration has on the relationships between male migrants and women who stay behind. Similarly, especially in areas where part of the community migrates while others do not, previously cohesive villages may develop splits with migrants being excluded from some forms of decision-making (as apparently occurs among some Bhil communities in Gujarat[30]), and with more affluent members who do not migrate monopolising resources[31]. In place of earlier identities, a sense of identity tends to develop among the migrant workers with one another, as was the case among Warli adivasis in Thane district. Caste identities may both be reinforced in this fashion, when the same caste migrates together, and also crossed, when multiple sub-castes work in the same area (as was described for Bengal above).

Finally, not all migration results in no change in the standard of living of migrant workers themselves. In Bengal, for instance, about one quarter of migrants in some streams of migration into Barddhaman district returned with sufficient savings to lease land, purchase livestock or buy small areas of land[32]. In Andhra Pradesh, migrants who worked on sugarcane cutting and negotiated directly with their employers were able to save significant amounts of money, while others who worked as specialised diggers for telephone cables and other earthworks were able to purchase land, build pucca houses and drill wells with their savings[33]. However, none of these changes implied any significant shift in class position – even those who were able to invest in land were mostly not able to buy enough as to cease working for wages, or even to cease migrating.

But these examples are far from random. The minority of cases in which migration of this kind takes place share two common characteristics. In the first place, those who accumulated in this fashion typically were not landless workers – they were marginal peasants with some control over resources and access to means of production, meaning that wage labour was not their only source of survival and hence they were (presumably) not already trapped in an intensifying cycle of debt. The second condition was the existence of conditions that allowed for migrant workers to, in one way or another, *de facto* (even if not consciously) organise themselves. In the cable digging example given for

Andhra Pradesh above, the work was skilled in nature and identified with a specific caste, which in turn was able to form a cooperative society and negotiate with employers. In Bengal, the strong presence of political parties in the destination Barddhaman district (including but not only the CPI(M)) and a relative shortage of workers combined to create minimal mechanisms whereby workers could try to enforce a uniform wage and make sure wages were paid. The Krishak Sabha, for instance, sought to protect local workers and the "reputation" of the destination villages by supporting migrant workers who sought the wage that had been earlier fixed for the area. Such mechanisms may have failed most of the time, but their existence still provided a minimal base for workers to resist. This is a point to which we will return in greater depth in chapter 4, when exploring the implications of migrant labour for the national and regional political economy.

References

1. In contrast, in Brazil, for instance, certain communities live in cities and migrate during the agricultural seasons. See Standing 1981.
2. Deshingkar and Start 2003.
3. Deshingkar and Start 2003.
4. Rogaly and Rafique 2003.
5. For discussions of these processes, see Patnaik 1983, Breman 2008 and Chapter 4.
6. Mosse et al 2002.
7. A more detailed discussion on these changes can be found in Rao 1999.
8. See Deshingkar and Start 2003, Rogaly 2003 for examples.
9. Mosse et al 2002.
10. Deshingkar and Start 2003.
11. Sharma 2005.
12. Rogaly and Coppard 2003.
13. Rogaly and Coppard 2003.
14. Sharma 2005.
15. Da Corta and Venkateshwarlu 1999.

16. For instance, in Bengal (Rogaly and Coppard 2003), in Bihar (Sharma 2005), and in Andhra Pradesh (Deshingkar and Start 2003).
17. Rogaly and Rafique 2003.
18. Rogaly and Coppard 2003.
19. Breman 2008.
20. As in sugarcane cutting in Gujarat – see Breman 2008.
21. Deshingkar and Start 2003.
22. Smita 2008.
23. Da Corta and Venkateshwarlu 1999.
24. Rogaly and Rafique 2003.
25. Rogaly and Rafique 2003, Mosse et al 2002.
26. Da Corta and Venkateshwarlu 1999.
27. Rogaly and Coppard 2003.
28. Da Corta and Venkateshwarlu 1999.
29. A more detailed exploration of this argument is discussed by Standing (1981).
30. Mosse et al 2002.
31. Smita 2008.
32. Rogaly and Rafique 2003.
33. Deshingkar and Start 2003.

Chapter II

The Site of Destination

If sites of origin of migration are varied, the sites of destination – where workers go to work – are even more so. Seasonal migrants go to a range of different work sites, at different distances and under different conditions; and this is to say nothing of the variety of different places to which long term migrants or very short term commuter migrant workers are drawn. Each of these locations has its own dynamics. This chapter therefore presents a brief overview, identifying some of the common features across these different areas.

Some Types of Worksites

We can broadly divide worksites into two categories: non-agricultural and agricultural.

Non-Agricultural Work

The majority of seasonal migration is to non-agricultural work sites, most of which are in rural or semi-urban areas. One estimate says that only 15% of migrants from Bihar migrated for agricultural work[1]. Migration to urban worksites also takes place on a seasonal basis, though a large proportion of those who migrate to urban areas do so on a long term basis, as the work in urban areas is less likely to be seasonal in nature. Among the well known non-agricultural migrant labour worksites are the following:

- Construction and earthworks

- Salt pans
- Brick kilns
- Stone quarrying
- Mining
- Fishing

The employers in such worksites vary widely. At one extreme are very large corporations, such as the employers in many construction sites (including public sector corporations and multinationals), who hire migrant workers through a chain of contractors. At the other are small and petty producers who may hire their workers directly from nearby villagers. In between come the medium and small producers such as brick kiln owners, salt pan owners etc.

Migration for this kind of work tends to be longer in duration, often extending to more than six months and covering the entire non-agricultural season at the site of origin. In Thane District, for instance, migrants would depart from their homes soon after Diwali and return at the time of Holi. A large portion of the year, in some cases most of the year, is spent at the worksite.

Agricultural Work

Seasonal migration for agricultural work typically involves migrating to areas of cash crop farming, and therefore of agricultural capitalism. Labour demand peaks during the harvest season, and large numbers of migrant workers frequently come to such areas during these seasonal periods. For instance, more than 5,00,000 people migrate into Barddhaman district in central West Bengal every year for the rice harvests, doubling the local workforce[2]. Approximately 6,50,000 workers are estimated to migrate to western Maharashtra every year for the sugarcane harvest[3], while around 50,000 (now probably much higher) workers migrated from the same areas to Gujarat for this work in the 1970's[4].

Migration for agricultural work varies from long term

migration similar to that in non-agricultural employment (such as in the case of sugar cane cutting), to short term migration of a few weeks, several times a year, in other areas (such as in the case of migration from some areas for rice cultivation in West Bengal).

The employers in these cases are generally agricultural capitalists, either operating as individual landlords and rich peasants[5], or as organised cooperatives, as in sugarcane cultivation. However, while in most cases such capitalists operate as the primary driving engine of employing migrant labour, other peasant classes also do so. In Bengal, for instance, many small and middle peasants also hire migrant workers, and poor peasants do so too at the peak of rice cultivation; all these classes do so by "borrowing" them from larger landlords[6]. In such sites of destination, small producers therefore occupy multiple class positions, hiring in migrant workers during the harvest season and frequently hiring themselves out as workers during other seasons[7].

Characteristics of the Worksites

Despite the wide range of worksites, however, there are some common characteristics that are shared by most worksites that are sites of destination for migrant workers. These include the following.

Seasonal, Short-Term and Insecure Employment

By definition, of course, employment of seasonal migrant workers is short term and seasonal in nature. It is rare for workers to return to the same worksite year after year, and in most cases the employment is based on a contract that applies only to the current season. In such circumstances the work is also mostly unskilled in nature, implying that the employer does not require the same workers to return.

While this might seem inevitable given the nature of the kind of work that hires migrant workers, as discussed later in this chapter and in chapter 4, this kind of employment is at least partly the *result* of the existence of migrant labour.

Layered Management of the Work Process

Excepting in the case of petty producers or middle peasants, in many migration work sites the management of the workers is done through their *thekedars* or contractors (see next section). Rather than the employer directly managing workers, this function is "outsourced" to the thekedars, who take responsibility for a team of workers under their control. Direct contact with the employer is minimised or non-existent, as in work for the sugar cooperatives in Gujarat[8] or work on most construction sites. It is common on many construction worksites for the workers to not even know who the ultimate employer is. These structures are discussed more in the next section.

Isolation from the Local Population

A second key feature of most sites of destination is the isolation that is maintained between the migrant workforce and the local population. At times this isolation is the result of being physically remote, as in fishwork, mines or stone quarries. But even where the work site is in a densely populated area, deliberate steps are taken – especially by the owners, but also frequently by the local population itself – to minimise contacts between the migrant workers and others. Jan Breman (1978) describes in detail how migrant workers in the southern Gujarat sugarcane fields are given shelter next to the fields themselves and were essentially unable to contact anyone in the area. Similarly, in urban contexts and in construction worksites, clearly demarcated areas are allocated to migrant workers. This becomes a key facilitator of exploitation, as discussed in the next section.

Preference for Migrant Workers

Capitalists and government agencies frequently describe the use of migrant workers as a reflection of a "shortage of labour" in the local area, or because the local workers are "unsuitable." In fact this is usually a myth. For instance, in brick kiln works where adviasis migrated in Maharashtra, local women would not be hired even to fetch water or to cook food; migrant women would be paid instead. Similarly, Breman (1978, 2008) clearly demonstrated how there was no shortage of workers in Gujarat for sugarcane cutting and other harvesting activities, and indeed the local landless Halpati community were underemployed.

These stories are not unique to those areas; indeed, agricultural worksites are often in areas with a high degree of capitalist agriculture, and are therefore precisely the areas with higher inequality and landlessness. The same is true of many construction and industrial projects, where it is known that employers will not hire local workers, including for instance those displaced by land acquisition for the project.

The "shortage", in other words, results not from any lack of local workers but arises because the capitalists actively *prefer* to hire migrant workers. The result is often a cycle of migration, where people from one area migrate to another, while the local workers of the destination area are themselves required to migrate elsewhere for work, etc.

Why would local capitalists prefer migrant workers over local workers? Clearly, because the former are easier to control. This brings us to the key question of the site of destination: namely the methods by which migrant workers are exploited. This is the question to which we turn next.

Structures of Exploitation of Migrant Workers

Migrant workers are perhaps the most extensively exploited sector of the entire unorganised sector workforce in India today. Multiple methods are used to ensure a maximum of extraction of surplus from these workers.

Piece Rate Wages and Lump Sum Payments

Wages for migrant labour are often paid on the basis of piece rates. As in such piece rates of contracts in most unorganised sector work in India, the required quantum of work is inevitably too high for workers to complete, forcing them to work intensively for extended hours in order to earn enough to survive. Migrant workers from Murshidabad, West Bengal, may work from 2 am till 10 pm at night during rice harvest seasons[9]. Piece rates also transfer the risks of production failure on to the workers; the costs of equipment breakdowns, the interruption of rains during the harvest, or other problems that prevent production from being completed, are all borne by the workers.

The wages that are earned are frequently paid as a lump sum at the end of the season, before workers return. At most, as in the brick kilns and salt pans in Maharashtra, workers are paid small amounts every week in order to allow them to survive (and such amounts may then be calculated as "advances"). Lump sum payments in themselves reduce workers' ability to resist, since they cannot leave the worksite or the employer until the end of the season, no matter how atrocious the working conditions, unless they are prepared to lose their wages. This is particularly damaging in worksites where workers stay for extended periods of several months.

The system of lump sum payments also provides the capitalist with a method of escape. It is common for employers to vanish when the time for payments comes due, or to pay less than the agreed amount, knowing that in most cases migrant workers have no recourse, being entirely dependent on the employer for shelter and survival. Workers who are hired from nakas and labour markets in particular often do not even know where they have been taken to or who the ultimate employer is, making it very easy to cheat them.

Workers in such circumstances frequently have to beg their way home. Since, as said above, most work does not require skilled or repeat workers, such employers need not even be concerned that the workers will not return the next year – others will inevitably be available.

Advances on Wages

In addition, a further common practice is for the contractor or the employer to pay a paltry advance on the workers' wages in the form of a loan. Such loans are often vital to cover the costs of inputs for cultivation during the agricultural season[10]. As noted in the previous chapters, since it is difficult to get loans from other sources, especially for landless workers, loans are most often taken as advances. These advances are then deducted from the workers' wages after the season. These advances, as noted earlier, have the effect of "tying" the worker to the employer, preventing the worker from going to any other employer, contractor or work site. The advance amounts can also be easily manipulated when wages are actually paid, since workers usually have no record. This allows the employer to deduct large amounts and at times the workers leave with almost no payment at all.

Lack of Shelter and Facilities

The migrant workers are entirely dependent on their employer for shelter and basic supplies, as well as on the traders who frequently set up shop near migrant worksites. Shelter rarely consists of anything more than a plastic sheet and a few poles at most. The capitalists often deduct the "costs" of this shelter from wages, inflating the costs in the process and thereby further reducing the actual wage that is paid. The same applies to basic food supplies, such as rice and foodgrains, cooking oil, etc. In salt pan works in Maharashtra, migrants were often supplied with food by the employer on loan, or else purchased it out of the "advances" paid to them before the final lump sum payment. The food was then cooked by the workers in the afternoons. Otherwise, food has to be bought from surrounding traders. These traders in turn also hike their prices, since the migrant workers have few options[11]. In the case where workers are employed through contractors or *thekedars* (see next chapter), shelter supplies and wage payments are frequently made to the contractor by the employer, and the contractor then takes a further cut before supplying them to the workers.

The net result is that the extreme dependency of the workers is used to extract further gains from them not only by the capitalists, but also by other actors who can exploit the workers in the area.

Unpaid or Low Wage Work by Family Members

As members of the community often migrate as family units, capitalists receive the labour of the entire family, often in exchange for paying a single wage to the male migrant worker. Where women are paid for their work, these wages are always lower than those of the male workers. Children are rarely if ever paid, but join the work in almost all circumstances[12]. Frequently this is ensured by setting piece rates so low, or the quantum of one unit of work so high, that the entire family has to work in order to ensure sufficient wages[13].

Lack of State Welfare and Legal Protection

Even the limited state welfare systems, legal protections etc. that exist for most workers in India do not exist for seasonal migrant workers. Being mobile and away from their place of residence, they cannot access the local ration shops[14], cannot enroll their children in the local schools, and often have no access to local health care facilities. The police and labour inspectorates are largely inaccessible and in any case entirely on the side of the local capitalists, who are after all the local dominant community[15]. India's labour laws contain few provisions for protection of migrants and do not recognise migrant labour as a separate category. The isolation of migrants from the local population prevents them further from building any network in the local community for survival. Together these phenomena ensure that the dependence on the contractor and/or the capitalist is total and the possibilities of resistance slim.

Sexual Exploitation of Women

In addition to their exploitation as workers, sexual molestation and assaults on women by employers, contractors and at times fellow migrants is also extremely common. Moreover, migrating women may be forced into sex work in order to survive; a recent newspaper report for instance cited a survey that found that 25% of women migrant workers in Raigad's construction areas were sex workers[16].

Labour Relations at the Worksites

The exploitative structures described above can be summed up in the fact that *all* spaces of security and collective action are denied to most migrant workers by the simple fact that they are not local workers. Indeed, the capitalists do not even pay sufficient amounts for them to survive as human beings, and hence their survival becomes conditional on their return to their home area on a seasonal basis. Thus the cost of reproduction of the workforce is essentially subsidised for the capitalists by the site of origin. The result is a drain on the site of origin and on the means of production of workers and their families in order to cheapen labour costs for the capitalists at the site of destination.

The extreme nature of this extraction of resources is indicated by the fact that any change in the conditions of workers that permits them even minimal control over their work relationship – such as the intervention of political parties in West Bengal as discussed in the previous chapter. Yet such conditions are rare, and instead the scope of migration continues to grow. The impact of such processes on the larger economy are discussed in chapter 4. But before entering that analysis, there is a further process that has to be discussed, namely how migration itself is organised.

References

1. Sharma 2005.
2. Rogaly and Coppard 2003.
3. Smita 2008.
4. Breman 1978.
5. As is the case in West Bengal; see Rogaly 1998.
6. Rogaly and Coppard 2003.
7. This situation is true of much of Indian agriculture as a whole, as argued in Patnaik 1983.
8. Breman 1978.
9. Rogaly and Rafique 2003.
10. See for instance Mosse et al 2002 on Bhils in Gujarat.
11. Breman 1978 gives some examples of this practice.
12. See Breman 1978, Breman 2008, Smita 2008, Deshingkar and Start 2000 etc. for examples.
13. Breman 1978.
14. Smita 2008.
15. Breman 1994.
16. Shetty 2009.

Chapter III

The Process of Migration

The general impression produced by official policy literature, as well as the common idea of migration among people not familiar with the ground reality, is that migration is highly disorganised and consists of people flocking to worksites looking for work. In reality this is entirely untrue. In most cases, the seasonal migration process is tightly organised, often coordinated from the point of recruiting the worker to the point where the worker returns home. The control over this process and the manner in which it is constructed play a key part in determining the political, social and economic impact of migration.

Recruitment of Migrant Workers

The recruitment of migrant workers typically takes place through one of four methods[1]:

- Through a *thekedar* (also known in some areas as a *sardar, mukkadam* or by other local terms), essentially a local job contractor.
- Through previous or current employment by kin in that area.
- Through hiring of workers at *nakas* or specific casual labour markets.
- Direct hiring by the employer from the village.

Each of these methods has different implications for the workers' relationship with one another and with capital. We explore these implications below.

Recruitment Through a Thekedar

The most common method of recruiting migrant labour is through a *thekedar*, who acts as the intermediary between the capitalist (or between a next level of contractor) and the worker. In some areas, though not always, *thekedars* are members of the village and former migrant workers themselves. Where thekedars are used, they usually not only identify and recruit the workers, but also act as managers of the work and agents of the employer.

For instance, in sugarcane cutting by sugar cooperatives in Gujarat, the thekedars serve multiple roles. They identify workers in the villages to hire, based on personal, family and caste connections, and report the numbers of workers they can provide to the cooperative. Advances are paid to the thekedar for payment to the workers. The thekedars travel to the work site with the workers, and, once there, all supplies and payments to the workers go through the thekedar. The thekedar in turn is obliged to ensure that work quotas are completed on time and to distribute work between the workers under him. The cooperative in fact never deals directly with the workers at all, except on the rare occasion when the management gets involved in disputes between the workers and the thekedar[2].

Thekedars also serve other functions. In some areas, thekedars are not agents of just one employer, but instead are in touch with several employers and recruit labourers for them. Thus among Bhil adivasis in southern Gujarat, thekedars act as moneylenders, offering loans during the cultivation season as advances on wage payments. A thekedar in such circumstances has to also have the confidence of the workers as being someone who can secure work[3].

The figure of the thekedar plays a complex role in labour relations with migrant workers. As essentially a subcontractor, he is an agent of the capitalist whose interest lies in extracting the maximum amount of labour from the workers, and hence in suppressing resistance and collective action by the workers. Through the thekedar, the capitalist saves on management costs and secures maximum extraction of labour without any direct effort.

Yet, the thekedar also has a different relationship with the workers than purely that of an employer. The workers depend on the thekedars for both present and future employment, a thekedar cannot easily be targeted. Moreover, since thekedars may be members of the community and former workers themselves, it is difficult for migrant workers to organise against thekedars as a group. Instead, workers identify their interests with finding the best thekedar (where a choice is available) and then trying to ensure that the thekedar does not cheat them and secures work for them.

Previous or Current Work by Kin in the Area

Finding work through kin is frequently seen as the most secure option for migrant workers, and characterises some of the migration streams where savings are possible[4]. This is partly a reflection of the fact that such a system can operate only where the employer themselves has an interest in the continuance of particular workers, for otherwise kin connections are of little value. This applies in skilled labour work or where employers develop long term relations with migrant workers in order to easily secure labour in areas or at times of labour shortage. By their very nature, such forms of migrant work are inherently more predictable and offer more security, and hence the possibility of demanding better conditions. Kin groups are also able to act in a more collective fashion, to travel together and to support one another during crises. Accessing such kin groups, however, requires both that this kind of work exists and that the worker has access to such a kin group – workers may be excluded due to their reputation, lack of assets (which means they cannot help other members of the group when required), etc[5].

Hiring of Workers at Nakas and Markets

In some areas, and among some workers, workers attempt to be hired at a naka by an employer or a contractor, rather than to go through a thekedar or a kin network. This tends to be more common with short term migration, and is for instance the standard method of recruitment for migrants for rice cultivation in Murshidabad[6]. In other areas, it can reflect both a higher degree of security – meaning that the worker can risk more in the hope of a better wage – or a lack of access to any other network[7]. In such cases the contract is usually struck on the spot with the migrant worker. However, in such situations, migrant workers often find themselves at a disadvantage and are unable to demand the full specification of the contract[8], particularly on issues other than wages – such as food supply, shelter, etc. While there is often a cash payment on the spot, this increases vulnerability to increased exploitation later in the contract, as frequently occurred in Murshidabad.

Direct Hiring in the Village

The last form of recruitment, which is direct hiring in the village by the capitalist, tends to occur where the employer is a middle peasant or small producer and requires work for the short term.

The Impact of the Migration Process on Collective Action

Despite these differences between different forms of recruitment and organising of migration, there are common features. The most common methods of recruiting workers, namely thekedars and family networks, both mean that workers get access to work on the basis of *who they know* as a result of caste, personal or family identity. Instead of workers accessing work through a wage labour relationship where capitalists offer a certain wage, workers access work through asserting their identity as a member of one or the other network.

Economists refer to this as "segmenting the labour market." This fragments workers on lines other than their class identity as workers. Thus, the common interest of the workers is limited to those in that network, and they have no short term interest in joining with all other migrant workers. Instead, they have a short term interest in finding a good thekedar and ensuring that the relationship with that thekedar continues. It is better for a worker to tie up with a particular thekedar than to organise with other workers generally, for to do the latter is to risk one's connection with the thekedar and hence with employment.

For capitalists, too, such methods of recruiting migrant labour work well. They can secure workers with little expense and generally without competing with each other. This is not always true, and indeed the opposite takes place in the rice growing areas of Barddhaman district in Bengal[9]. But in general, the network of thekedars and kin groups ensures that workers are fragmented and cannot seek out employment by comparing how much each capitalist is willing to pay. Instead, workers have little choice in where they go, since they are tied to one or the other group and that decision is taken by others (the thekedar). Often workers may not even know who their ultimate employer is. As a result, capitalists can keep wages low, since workers in any case cannot choose one capitalist over the other.

Direct hiring at nakas or in the village presents different problems with similar consequences. Lacking any security of employment, those who undertake migration through these processes will often not be with the same employer or even with the same workers in the next migration season. Resistance in this context becomes very difficult to organise, as there is no security for employment.

The net result is a highly fragmented working class, a result that, as the next chapter seeks to explore, plays a key role in the long term role of migration in the Indian social formation as such.

References

1. Compiled from Mosse et al 2002 and other reports cited in this study, as well as experience of one of the authors.
2. This is drawn from Breman 1978.
3. Mosse et al 2002.
4. Deshingkar and Start 2003.
5. Mosse et al 2002.
6. Rogaly and Rafique 2003.
7. Mosse et al 2002.
8. Rogaly and Rafique 2003.
9. Rogaly 1998.

Chapter IV

The Larger Social Formation

Throughout this study we have argued that all of the above processes – the developments at the site of origin, the structures at the site of destination and the process of migration itself – are not accidental but rather facets of a larger social formation at work. This chapter takes a brief look at some aspects of this larger process, asking how these structures have developed. What we argue here is that the social relations discussed in the previous chapters are the result of regional / national processes which have made it advantageous to Indian capital to generate crisis at one point (at sites of origin), a distorted "employment" at another (the sites of destination) and a particular kind of migration process that connects the two and makes it possible for the whole system to function. What looks like a problem faced by each migrant worker because of landlessness and low employment is in fact something produced by more than a hundred years of India's history. We cannot fight it if we do not see it within these larger changes.

Creating a Reserve Army of Labour: Transitions in Agriculture

In the discussion in chapter 1 on sites of origin, two key issues were identified as problems in rural areas: rising landlessness and the need for a cash income. The two phenomena are closely linked, and rooted in the transformation of Indian agriculture since the 19th century. Marxist and other analysts have long debated the nature of this transition. That debate is too large an issue to be addressed in this booklet, but there are a few trends that can be identified, and which directly link into the conditions in the home areas of migrant workers that we discussed in chapter 1.

While change processes in some areas were already underway, a key point of transition occurred during the colonial period in many areas of Indian agriculture. Some of the changes included[1]:

- Land was made into legally private property, that could be bought, sold, formally rented, etc.;
- A money tax was imposed that had to be paid in the period *before* the harvest;
- The possibility of selling cash crops internally and through exports increased as the colonial authorities introduced transportation infrastructure;
- Irrigation works were attempted in some areas and incentives given for commercial crops, and in some areas people were even forced to switch to commercial crops needed by the British;
- Since land could be bought and sold, money lending against land became common.

The net result of all of these changes was to force people into an increasing need for cash. For instance, by imposing taxes that had to be paid before the harvest, when farmers would have less money at hand, the colonial authorities forced practically all cultivators to take loans. Only those cultivators who had large landholdings and were cultivating sufficient cash crops as to create a surplus could escape the resulting cycle of interest payments, more loans and hence eventually a debt trap. Simultaneously, allowing land to be bought and sold meant that loans could now be given against land. In such cases, the smaller peasants and marginal cultivators in some cases (though far from all) lost their land entirely, and in all cases were forced into seeking to earn cash

– either through cultivation of cash crops, which would not be sufficient except for those with large holdings, or through seeking employment.

This dynamic continued over the decades that followed, and drove large numbers of people into performing agricultural labour. In British India, between 1891 and 1931, the proportion of agricultural labourers rose from 13% of the agricultural population to 30%[2]. This trend accelerated after Independence, with one major reason for the continuation of the process being the manner in which zamindari abolition and tenancy laws were implemented in India. There were two familiar features of these laws that led to these consequences. First, zamindari abolition laws did not require that the zamindars always give up the land – instead, they said that the zamindars could be declared owners of lands that they cultivated with their own hired labour (as opposed to those that were cultivated by tenants). Similarly, the tenancy legislations varied in their recognition of tenancy rights, but almost always made it difficult to recognise tenancy contracts that were not written and provided that the tenant could purchase the land vested in the government upon payment of a multiple of land revenue.

The result was that there was large scale eviction of small tenants from zamindars' lands (in order to show that the zamindar was directly cultivating the land), most tenancies were never recorded or recognised, and meanwhile only the small number of rich peasant tenants could actually purchase the land vested in the government. Those evicted and those who lost their tenancies were also forced to sell their labour to survive and joined the ranks of the landless labourers[3]. Meanwhile, the lack of implementation of the land ceiling laws and the failure to distribute land meant that most landlords managed to retain control of very large parts of their land, and the land reforms failed to provide small and marginal peasants, or landless workers, with sufficient land to produce cash crops or a surplus that could allow them to survive without selling their labour.

Further developments also drove the changes in the structure of employment relations that we discussed in chapter 1. India has always had landless communities who survived by working for others[4], but such work was frequently done in the form of a "patron client" relationship, where the workers were attached on a personal or caste basis to a particular zamindar, landlord or other employer for life. Even as the number of those seeking employment increased, such relationships continued to exist and dominate in many areas. As discussed in Chapter 1, while forming a brutal and forcible method of extracting labour from people, these kinds of 'traditional' labour relationships also offered a minimal degree of security – the landlord was expected to "help" the worker, there existed traditional obligations to provide workers with gifts and assistance with health and ceremonial expenses, etc.

The breakdown in these relations, and the shift to cash wages, was a result of multiple factors. First, the rapid increase in the number of landless labourers meant that landlords increasingly had no reason to enter into a traditional relationship of obligation – it would be easier to hire a worker on a cash basis for a defined period without incurring other, potentially permanent obligations. A second incentive that helped drive this tendency was the rising rate of inflation post independence in India. This inflation rate was the result of the government's policy of state-led development, with large-scale public spending, while at the same time the government failed to tax the landlords and large industrialists. This produced a situation where the government inevitably was overspending. Moreover, since most people lacked the income to purchase much goods, industrial capacity was also low. The result was that prices rose as more money entered the economy while actual production remained very low. Food prices in particular rose very fast. In this context, it was to the advantage of landlords and in fact of all employers to pay cash wages, since a fixed wage would over time have less and less value, even as the sale prices of cash food crops would keep rising[5].

Even as such trends were manifesting themselves among the general peasantry, similar developments took place among adivasis for slightly different reasons. The forest laws had already forced many adivasi communities to abandon shifting cultivation and other traditional forms, and instead to adopt settled cultivation of small plots of land, while remaining dependent on the forest for medicine, many foods and saleable items like honey. The increasing exploitation of these forest lands by the government, the restrictions in access from tightening forest laws, and the takeover of forest lands by zamindars and landlords, reduced access to these resources. The increasing population in adivasi communities occurred therefore at precisely the time when access to forest resources was falling. This, combined with the penetration of markets and exchange relations into these areas, pushed adivasis into a position where they too were increasingly required to participate in the cash economy and to purchase the essentials of survival. Meanwhile, throughout this entire period, land grabbing by non-adivasis deprived adivasis of large areas of land; as the dependence on the cash economy increased, much of this land grabbing took place through moneylending, driving a vicious cycle where adivasis lost more and more of their land and forest resources. Hence it is no surprise that most adivasi communities report "deforestation" and "too little land" as a major reason for their need to work, and, hence, their need to migrate.

These transitions hence created a situation where a very large number of people in rural areas engage in wage labour for survival. It is important to note that this was not a result purely either of local issues, or of one or the other failed policy. For instance, it did not happen only because the tenancy laws were not implemented properly, or because the forest laws deprived adivasis of their rights. The changes that have occurred are much larger than that, and revolved around a transition in how both land and people are involved in production relations. It is this that produces the desperation for work that marks rural India today, and which is the first and most fundamental reason that people eventually take up migration.

Finding Work in a Distorted Economy

The next question is where and how people need to find work. In chapter 1, we noted some of the immediate reasons that productive employment is difficult to find in most rural areas. These factors too are however deeply linked into the processes we described above. First, having been deprived of their security and most of their livelihood, small and marginal peasants and landless workers lack sufficient income and purchasing capacity to constitute a market for many goods. Hence, Indian capital has largely focused its entire productive capacity on a small portion of the population, producing the familiar distorted reality whereby infrastructure, industry and employment are all concentrated in certain small areas.

More importantly, however, the sheer existence of such a large "reserve army of labour" (as Marx called it) has its own impact on the capitalist production process. First, those who are able to accumulate some capital often find it far more profitable to lend it to the landless and small peasants than to use it to cultivate or to invest it in other productive activity. Such loans can often have extreme rates of interest and moreover can be linked to forcing people to lower their crop prices or their wages, allowing for further profits.

Second, even where capital is invested and people are employed, it is extremely easy to keep wages very low as there are frequently other workers available. Even if there is a relative shortage, it is possible to take advantage of workers' indebtedness to "tie" them to employment and keep wages low, since workers always need loans to cover slack seasons and times of low employment or low production[6].

This occurred in many areas during the 1970's and 1980's in India, the "Green Revolution" decades when capitalist farming was viable in many areas due to high cash crop prices and considerable support and subsidies from the state. Such high cash crop prices and the increased labour demand did not produce correspondingly high wages, and the rise in real wages of agricultural workers that did occur during this period was more attributable to the increased spending on public works[7]. After 1991, with the collapse in agricultural prices, even large farmers have been subjected to a "price squeeze" that has forced wages down further and led to a lack of overall employment.

The net result is that, in most of rural India, wages and consumption of the majority of people remain extremely low. In order to generate any degree of 'prosperity' in a capitalist economy, the surplus generated has to be reinvested in productive activity, that in turn employs people who consume the production with their wages. What happens in India instead is that surplus is extracted from workers and then either invested unproductively – as in moneylending – or reinvested out of the area entirely. The very existence of the enormous "reserve army of labour" is what allows this to continue.

What is the role of migration, particularly seasonal migration, in this scenario? As a result of the fact that capitalist production becomes concentrated in certain areas, people increasingly migrate in order to locate employment. But migration here is not just a result of the existing situation – it also plays a role in shaping it. Migration has multiple consequences for the overall political economy.

First, as discussed at the end of chapter 2, when migrant workers are employed in production, their exploitation is essentially subsidised by their homes – their lands, families and other means of survival that they have access to in their home areas. The costs of reproducing the workers are partly borne by the site of origin. In practice this amounts to a transfer of resources, material and human, from the site of origin to the capitalists of the site of destination. The costs are visible in many ways. Children of migrant workers who travel with them, for instance, almost never get an education, with their childhoods essentially granted as free labour to the capitalists. Families of migrant workers that stay behind have to rely on their relatives for survival, and often on further loans that act as a burden on their ability to survive. The ability of the migrants to participate in community activities and in maintaining common resources during the non-agricultural season is lost, resulting in the destruction or damage to those resources in areas where most or all of the community migrates. In some cases, migration even clashes with the end or beginning of the agricultural season in the home area, with some workers forced to leave due to the need for cash[8].

Second, migration operates as the extreme form of subjugation of labour. The extreme degree of control that capitalists exercise over migrant workers means that the cost of labour becomes extremely low for these capitalists, allowing the use of production methods and working conditions – like those in brick kilns, salt pans, and the construction industry – that would otherwise be impossible if only because they are so inhuman. The inability of migrant workers to resist means that there is no incentive for capitalists to invest in production practices that improve productivity, relying instead on what Marx described as the extraction of "absolute surplus value" to the maximum extent possible. This in turn means that wage goods remain relatively expensive for workers and destitution, in most cases, continues.

Migration As A Force for "Disorganising" Labour

But more important than these apparent effects, however, is the third and most fundamental consequence of migration:

the fact that *it effectively and thoroughly* ***disorganises*** *the workforce.*

What do we mean by this? In chapter 3, we discussed how the the process of migration – especially through *thekedars* and through family networks – means that workers are broken into different segments. Migration is always *particularistic,* related to one or the other local network of caste, community, kin, contractor or employer. A migrant worker's immediate interests are with his or her own network, not with other migrant workers as such. thekedars and contractors in particular operate to break up any possibility of unity between workers, since in practice any such unity poses a danger to a worker's livelihood. This is then compounded by the extreme dependence of the migrant worker on his or her employer and on his or her contractor during the period of migration, which makes it even more difficult to conceive of resisting exploitation as a group. There is little to be gained from unity and everything to be lost. Nor is this condition limited to Indian workers: one analysis of migrant workers in Brazil found that they were "surprisingly politically conservative"[9].

The inability of migrant workers to constitute what Marx called a "class for itself" - a class that is conscious of its class identity – is in sharp contrast to the ability of their employers, the capitalists, to do precisely that. It is extremely common for hirers of migrant workers to consciously or implicitly cooperate to make sure that they are not competing for the same workers, that all workers are uniformly exploited, and that wages are kept as low as possible. For instance, Breman (1978) describes in detail how sugar cooperatives in south Gujarat ensure that there was coordination between their members, and with other cooperatives, to make sure that the same conditions of exploitation prevailed everywhere. Where migrant workers attempt on a rare occasion to revolt, the police, the state machinery and the local dominant class all immediately unite against them.

Moreover, the disorganising effect of migration is not limited to the migrant workers alone. There is also the clear impact that migrant labour has on the local workforce. As discussed in chapter 2, employers and capitalists prefer migrant workers as they can be repressed and controlled far more easily than local workers. In practice, even though wages of migrant workers may not be much lower, they can be exploited to such a degree that local workers cannot compete beyond a point. This means that even the struggles of local workers can often be easily broken by rich peasants and landlords, who replace the local workers with migrants if the locals' demands become "too high."

Finally, this disorganising effect extends beyond class identity. Migration has a dissolving effect on local communities, preventing them from functioning as a unit except where most of the community migrates together. Moreover, since such community institutions are largely irrelevant to the struggles and problems people face during migration, they turn to others as protectors – thekedars, contractors, and, where they exist and operate, political parties. But with these others, the relationship is at an individual level, rarely at the level of the community or the class. The overall result is the weakening of any organisational framework beyond the individual and the family, since village level organisations can only be relevant during the non-migratory season.

References

1. Bharadwaj 1985.
2. Patnaik 1983.
3. Patnaik 1983.
4. Patnaik 1983.
5. Patnaik 1983.
6. Rao 1999.
7. Chandrasekhar and Ghosh 2000.
8. For instance in Bengal women and children in some areas leave early; Rogaly and Rafique 2003.
9. Standing 1981.

Conclusion

In a way, migration is both an effect and a cause. It is an effect of the distorted way in which capital has shaped the Indian economy and of the processes that have transformed Indian agriculture. In large areas of rural India, the need for land is combined with a need for cash, a result of the way in which people have been separated from the means of production and pushed into the market economy. Given such a situation at what we have called "sites of origin", people are left with little choice except to migrate, mostly for basic survival, but also if they wish to save or accumulate.

But today migration is also as much a cause of the situation. It plays an important role in making it possible for capital – be it large corporations, capitalist farmers or brick kiln owners – to produce in a way that exploits workers with incredible brutality. The more that people migrate, the more that this kind of exploitation grows, which in turn makes employment for local workers even more difficult. Migration has disarticulated and undermined the process of struggle against exploitation of our people, both as workers and as peasants. Migration links the exploitation at the site of origin and the exploitation at the site of destination, and for most migrant workers it intensifies both.

Is the answer, then, to "stop" migration by fighting for more local livelihoods? The processes that drive people into the cash economy cannot be fought at the local level alone.

We saw above that people were pushed into earning money and spending it because of dynamics that are very large. For instance we can fight locally to win back adivasi land stolen by non-adivasis, and to get land reform and tenancy laws implemented. But however strong our local struggles for land, we cannot fight inflation, we cannot fight for cheaper goods for people to live on, and we cannot fight for Indian capital to begin to invest in our areas. We can demand that the state do so, but we cannot change the distorted nature of the Indian economy itself. This does not in any sense mean that the struggle against the exploiters of the home area is not important. It only would imply that it is not enough.

Does this mean nothing can be done? No. It means that, if migration is a feature of Indian capitalism, it is capital that we must fight. And for this, migrant workers have to fight not only their landlords but also their employers. They have to organise as workers. To fight these struggles needs us to strengthen the ability of migrant workers to organise themselves and build their organisations as a *class*. In the last chapter we discussed how migration has its most profound effects through the manner in which it fragments and disorganises the working class. It is this effect that we must fight, and as we do, as it becomes possible, automatically the exploitation of migrant workers will decrease and capital will find its ability to super-exploit workers threatened. It is only through providing a framework of struggle, a framework of demands and a system of organising that emphasises the *common class interest* of migrant workers that we can begin the process of fighting for justice.

This in turn means building organizations for this purpose and the use of the available legal and political spaces to create a situation where migrant workers can organise together. Such organizations often begin at the home areas of migrant workers, where local groups are already strong and workers are able to more freely organize. But since it is difficult to affect migration from the home area alone, connections between organizations, and the building of larger federations, can also be crucial to organizing migrant workers across both worksites and home areas. The legal and policy tools that are available for this purpose are discussed in more detail in an accompanying booklet. Building such a movement offers us a way to respond to the problems created by migration, and the destructive effect it has on all of our struggles for livelihoods, for justice and for dignity.

Bibliography

Bharadwaj, Krishna. 1985. A view on commercialisation in Indian agriculture and the development of capitalism. *Journal of Peasant Studies* 12, no. 4: 7.

Breman, Jan. 1978. Seasonal Migration and Co-operative Capitalism: Crushing of Cane and of Labour by Sugar Factories of Bardoli. *Economic and Political Weekly* 13, no. 31/33 (August): 1317-1360.

Breman, Jan. 1994. *Wage Hunters and Gatherers*. New Delhi: Oxford University Press.

Breman, Jan. 2008. *The Jan Breman Omnibus*. New Delhi: Oxford University Press.

Byres, T. J. 1999. Rural labour relations in India: Persistent themes, common processes and differential outcomes. *Journal of Peasant Studies* 26, no. 2: 10.

Chandrasekhar, C.P and Ghosh, Jayati. 2001. *The Market That Failed*. New Delhi: Leftword Books.

da Corta, Lucia, and Davuluri Venkateshwarlu. 1999. Unfree relations and the feminisation of agricultural labour in Andhra Pradesh, 1970–95. *Journal of Peasant Studies* 26, no. 2: 71.

Deshingkar, Priya, and Daniel Start. 2003. *Seasonal Migration for Livelihoods in India: Coping, Accumulation and Exclusion*. Working Paper. London: Overseas Development Institute, August.

Marx, Karl, and Utsa Patnaik. 2007. *The Agrarian Question in Marx and His Successors*. New Delhi: Leftword.

David Mosse, Sanjeev Gupta, Mona Mehta, Vidya Shah, Julia fnms Rees, and KRIBP Project Team. 2002. Brokered livelihoods:

Debt, Labour Migration and Development in Tribal Western India. *Journal of Development Studies* 38 (June): 59-88.

Patnaik, Utsa. 1983. On the Evolution of the Class of Agricultural Labourers in India. *Social Scientist* 11, no. 7 (July): 3-24.

Rao, J. Mohan. 1999. Agrarian power and unfree labour. *Journal of Peasant Studies* 26, no. 2: 242.

Rogaly, Ben. 2008. Migrant Workers in the ILO's 'Global Alliance Against Forced Labour" Report: A Critique. *Third World Quarterly*.

Rogaly, Ben, and Abdur Rafique. 2003. Struggling to Save Cash: Seasonal Migration and Vulnerability in West Bengal, India. *Development & Change* 34, no. 4: 659.

Rogaly, Ben, and Daniel Coppard. 2003. 'They Used To Go to Eat, Now They Go to Earn': The Changing Meanings of Seasonal Migration from Puruliya District in West Bengal, India. *Journal of Agrarian Change* 3, no. 3 (July): 395-433.

Ben Rogaly, Daniel Coppard, Abdur Safique, Kumar Rana, Amrita Sengupta, and Jhuma Biswas. 2002. Seasonal Migration and Welfare/Illfare in Eastern India: A Social Analysis. *Journal of Development Studies* 38 (June): 89-114.

Sharma, Alakh. 2005. Agrarian Relations and Socio-Economic Change in Bihar. *Economic and Political Weekly*, March 5.

Shetty, Sukanya. 2009. Steeped in Ignorance and Nowhere to Flee from Stigma. *Indian Express*, January 18, Mumbai edition.

Smita. 2008. *Distress Seasonal Migration and Impact on Children's Education*. Create Pathways to Access Research Monograph. NUEPA, May. http://www.create-rpc.org/pdf_documents/PTA28.pdf.

Standing, Guy. 1981. Migration and modes of exploitation: Social origins of immobility and mobility. *Journal of Peasant Studies* 8, no. 2: 173.